The Tibetan Book of Days

A Journal with thoughts from Sogyal Rinpoche

HarperSanFrancisco

An Imprint of HarperCollins*Publishers*

To serve the world out of the dynamic union of wisdom and compassion would be to participate most effectively in the preservation of the planet. Masters of all the religious traditions on earth now understand that spiritual training is *essential* not solely for monks and nuns but for all people, whatever their faith or way of life. The nature of spiritual development is intensely practical, active, and effective. The danger we are all in together makes it essential now that we no longer think of spiritual development as a luxury but as a necessity for survival.

As a famous Tibetan teaching says: 'When the world is filled with evil, all mishaps should be transformed into the path of enlightenment.'

First published in the U.S.A. in 1997 by HarperSanFrancisco
Product design copyright © Random House UK Limited 1996
Text © Rigpa Fellowship 1996
Photographs © C Corona, Brian Beresford, Diane Barker, Mark Tracy, Anders Anderson, John Miles
and Robin Bath 1996

HarperCollins Web Site: http://www.harpercollins.com
Harper Collins®,   ® and HarperSanFrancisco™ are trademarks of Harper Collins Publishers Inc.

Whilst every effort has been made to ensure accuracy, the publishers cannot accept liability for any errors.
Set in Bernhard Modern

Printed and bound in Singapore
Designed by the Senate

ISBN 0-00-649174-X

Front cover illustration: Guru Rinpoche Thangka © Rigpa
Back cover illustration: Butter lamps in the Jokhang Temple © Tibet Image Bank/John Miles

PADMASAMBHAVA: 'LOOKS LIKE ME'

Padmasambhava, the 'Precious Master', 'Guru Rinpoche', is the founder of Tibetan Buddhism, and the Buddha of our time. It is believed that, on seeing this statue at Samye in Tibet, where it was made in the eighth century, he remarked, *'It looks like me,'* and then blessed it saying, *'Now it is the same as me!'*

UK
Rigpa
330 Caledonian Road
London N1 1BB
Tel: (0)171 700 0185
Fax: (0)171 609 6068

USA
Rigpa USA
PO Box 607
Santa Cruz
CA 95061-0607
Tel: 1(408) 454 9103
Fax: 1(408) 454 0917

Ireland
Dublin
2nd Floor
12 Wicklow Street
Dublin 2
Tel & fax:
353 (0) 1 454 0480

Allihies
Dzogchen Beara
Garranes
Allihies
West Cork
Tel: 353 (0) 27 730 32
Fax: 353 (0) 27 731 77

Australia
RIGPA
12/37 Nicholson Street
Balmain NSW 2041
Tel: 61 (0) 2 555 9952
Fax: 61 (0) 2 973 2029

India
Dzoghchen Monastery
Dhondenling
P.O. Tibetan Settlement
Kollegal Taluk
Dist. Mysore
Kamataka State

Sogyal Rinpoche

Sogyal Rinpoche was born in Tibet and raised as a son by one of the most revered spiritual teachers of this century, Jamyang Khyentse Chökyi Lodrö. After Jamyang Khyentse passed away, Rinpoche continued his spiritual education with Dudjom Rinpoche, Dilgo Khyentse Rinpoche and many other great masters. He studied at university in Delhi and Cambridge, and began to teach in the West in 1974. Rinpoche is the founder and spiritual director, along with H. E. Dzogchen Rinpoche of RIGPA, an international network of centers and groups that follow the teachings of the Buddha under his guidance.

France
Paris
RIGPA
Centre National
22 rue Burq
75018 Paris
Tel: 33 42 54 53 25
Fax: 33 42 54 00 19

Roqueredonde
Lerab Ling
L'Engayresque
34650
Roqueredonde
Tel: 33 67 44 41 99
Fax: 33 67 44 44 20

Germany
Berlin
RIGPA
Hasenheide 9
10967 Berlin
Tel: 49 (0) 30 694 6433
Fax: 49 (0) 30 694 6583

Munich
RIGPA
Nibelungenstr. 11
80639 München
Tel: 49 (0) 89 13 31 20
Fax: 49 (0) 89 8712164

Netherlands
Stichting RIGPA
Sint Agnietenstraat 22
1012 EG Amsterdam
Tel: 31 (0) 20 623 8022
Fax: 31 (0) 20 622 5154

Switzerland
RIGPA
PO Box 253
8059 Zurich
Tel & fax:
41 (0) 1 463 33 53

Having lived and taught in the West for more than twenty years, Rinpoche has developed a profound insight into the Western mind. His rare gift for communication cuts through cultural, religious, and psychological barriers, to reveal the essential truth of the Buddha's teaching. Both the ease and humour with which he teaches, and his very presence, open the hearts and minds of his audience to an intensely personal experience of their own true nature. All this, as well as the remarkable sucess of *The Tibetan Book of Living and Dying*, have made Rinpoche one of the most popular interpreters of Tibetan Buddhism in the modern world.

Rinpoche teaches widely in Europe, America, Australia and Asia, leading retreats, and giving a broad range of trainings based on his book which offers spiritual care for the living and dying. He has become among the most important Buddhist masters teaching today, considered by many senior Tibetan masters as having a special role to play in the future of Buddhism, in both the West and in the East.

1997 YEAR PLANNER

JANUARY

M	T	W	T	F	S	S
		1	2	3	4	5
6	7	8	9	10	11	12
13	14	15	16	17	18	19
20	21	22	23	24	25	26
27	28	29	30	31		

FEBRUARY

M	T	W	T	F	S	S
					1	2
3	4	5	6	7	8	9
10	11	12	13	14	15	16
17	18	19	20	21	22	23
24	25	26	27	28		

MARCH

M	T	W	T	F	S	S
31					1	2
3	4	5	6	7	8	9
10	11	12	13	14	15	16
17	18	19	20	21	22	23
24	25	26	27	28	29	30

APRIL

M	T	W	T	F	S	S
	1	2	3	4	5	6
7	8	9	10	11	12	13
14	15	16	17	18	19	20
21	22	23	24	25	26	27
28	29	30				

MAY

M	T	W	T	F	S	S
			1	2	3	4
5	6	7	8	9	10	11
12	13	14	15	16	17	18
19	20	21	22	23	24	25
26	27	28	29	30	31	

JUNE

M	T	W	T	F	S	S
30						1
2	3	4	5	6	7	8
9	10	11	12	13	14	15
16	17	18	19	20	21	22
23	24	25	26	27	28	29

JULY

M	T	W	T	F	S	S
	1	2	3	4	5	6
7	8	9	10	11	12	13
14	15	16	17	18	19	20
21	22	23	24	25	26	27
28	29	30	31			

AUGUST

M	T	W	T	F	S	S
				1	2	3
4	5	6	7	8	9	10
11	12	13	14	15	16	17
18	19	20	21	22	23	24
25	26	27	28	29	30	31

SEPTEMBER

M	T	W	T	F	S	S
1	2	3	4	5	6	7
8	9	10	11	12	13	14
15	16	17	18	19	20	21
22	23	24	25	26	27	28
29	30					

OCTOBER

M	T	W	T	F	S	S
		1	2	3	4	5
6	7	8	9	10	11	12
13	14	15	16	17	18	19
20	21	22	23	24	25	26
27	28	29	30	31		

NOVEMBER

M	T	W	T	F	S	S
					1	2
3	4	5	6	7	8	9
10	11	12	13	14	15	16
17	18	19	20	21	22	23
24	25	26	27	28	29	30

DECEMBER

M	T	W	T	F	S	S
1	2	3	4	5	6	7
8	9	10	11	12	13	14
15	16	17	18	19	20	21
22	23	24	25	26	27	28
29	30	31				

1998 YEAR PLANNER

JANUARY

M	T	W	T	F	S	S
			1	2	3	4
5	6	7	8	9	10	11
12	13	14	15	16	17	18
19	20	21	22	23	24	25
26	27	28	29	30	31	

FEBRUARY

M	T	W	T	F	S	S
						1
2	3	4	5	6	7	8
9	10	11	12	13	14	15
16	17	18	19	20	21	22
23	24	25	26	27	28	

MARCH

M	T	W	T	F	S	S
30	31					1
2	3	4	5	6	7	8
9	10	11	12	13	14	15
16	17	18	19	20	21	22
23	24	25	26	27	28	29

APRIL

M	T	W	T	F	S	S
		1	2	3	4	5
6	7	8	9	10	11	12
13	14	15	16	17	18	19
20	21	22	23	24	25	26
27	28	29	30			

MAY

M	T	W	T	F	S	S
				1	2	3
4	5	6	7	8	9	10
11	12	13	14	15	16	17
18	19	20	21	22	23	24
25	26	27	28	29	30	31

JUNE

M	T	W	T	F	S	S
1	2	3	4	5	6	7
8	9	10	11	12	13	14
15	16	17	18	19	20	21
22	23	24	25	26	27	28
29	30					

JULY

M	T	W	T	F	S	S
		1	2	3	4	5
6	7	8	9	10	11	12
13	14	15	16	17	18	19
20	21	22	23	24	25	26
27	28	29	30	31		

AUGUST

M	T	W	T	F	S	S
31					1	2
3	4	5	6	7	8	9
10	11	12	13	14	15	16
17	18	19	20	21	22	23
24	25	26	27	28	29	30

SEPTEMBER

M	T	W	T	F	S	S
	1	2	3	4	5	6
7	8	9	10	11	12	13
14	15	16	17	18	19	20
21	22	23	24	25	26	27
28	29	30				

OCTOBER

M	T	W	T	F	S	S
			1	2	3	4
5	6	7	8	9	10	11
12	13	14	15	16	17	18
19	20	21	22	23	24	25
26	27	28	29	30	31	

NOVEMBER

M	T	W	T	F	S	S
30						1
2	3	4	5	6	7	8
9	10	11	12	13	14	15
16	17	18	19	20	21	22
23	24	25	26	27	28	29

DECEMBER

M	T	W	T	F	S	S
1	2	3	4	5	6	
7	8	9	10	11	12	13
14	15	16	17	18	19	20
21	22	23	24	25	26	27
28	29	30	31			

January

1

2

3

During a ceremony for his long life at the
Namgyal Monastery, Dharamsala, His
Holiness the Dalai Lama sits in front of the
impressive statues of Avalokiteshvara – the
Buddha of Compassion, and Guru Rinpoche,
who established Buddhism in Tibet.

January

4

5

6

7

8

To be a spiritual warrior means to develop a
special kind of courage, one that is innately
intelligent, gentle, and fearless.

January

9

10

11

12

13

Whatever we have done with our lives makes us what we are when we die. And everything, absolutely everything, counts.

January

14

15

16

17

18

'Whatever joy there is in this world
All comes from desiring others to be happy,
And whatever suffering there is in this world
All comes from desiring myself to be happy.'

SHANTIDEVA

January

19

20

21

22

23

In meditation, be at ease, be as natural and spacious as possible. Slip quietly out of the noose of your habitual anxious self, release all grasping, and relax into your true nature.

January

24

25

26

27

28

The purpose of meditation is to awaken in us
the skylike nature of mind, and to introduce
us to that which we really are, our unchanging
pure awareness that underlies the whole of life
and death.

January

29

30

31

For six years Prince Shakyamuni, the Buddha
to be, lived as an ascetic. His body, emaciated
by the austerities he went through, is depicted
here in this famous sculpture displayed in the
Lahore Museum, Pakistan.

February

1

2

3

4

5

If you were to draw one essential message from the fact of reincarnation, it would be: Develop a good heart, that longs for other beings to find lasting happiness, and acts to secure that happiness. Nourish and practice kindness.

February

6

7

8

9

10

The most important thing is not to get trapped in what I see everywhere in the West, a 'shopping mentality:' shopping around from master to master, teaching to teaching, without any continuity or real, sustained dedication to any one discipline.

February

11

12

13

14

15

How many of us are swept away by what I have come to call an 'active laziness'? It consists of cramming our lives with compulsive activity, so that there is no time at all to confront the real issues.

February

16

17

18

19

20

Whenever doubt arises, see it simply as an obstacle, recognise it as an understanding that is calling out to be clarified or unblocked, and know that it is not a fundamental problem, but simply a stage in the process of purification and learning.

February

21

22

23

24

25

Everything is inextricably interrelated: We come to realise we are responsible for everything we do, say, or think, responsible in fact for ourselves, everyone and everything else, and the entire universe.

February

26

27

28

29

This highly revered statue of Akshobya Vajra, a
representation of Shakyamuni Buddha at the
age of eight, is in the Ramoche Temple, Lhasa.
It was brought to Tibet in the 7th century as
part of the dowry of Bhrikuti, the Nepalese
wife of King Songsten Gampo.

March

1

2

3

4

5

'If you spent one-tenth of the time you devoted to distractions, like chasing women or making money, to spiritual practice, you would be enlightened in a few years!'

RAMAKRISHNA

March

6

7

8

9

10

In Tibetan, the word for body is *lü*, which means 'something you leave behind,' like baggage. Each time we say '*lü*,' it reminds us that we are only travellers, taking temporary refuge in this life and this body.

March

11

12

13

14

15

There is a famous saying: 'If the mind is not contrived, it is spontaneously blissful, just as water, when not agitated, is by nature transparent and clear.'

March

16

17

18

19

20

Difficulties and obstacles, if properly understood and used, can turn out to be an unexpected source of strength.

March

21

22

23

24

25

If we are interdependent with everything and everyone else, even our smallest, least significant thought, work and action have real consequences throughout the universe.

March

26

27

28

29

Death is a vast mystery, but there are two things we can say about it: *It is absolutely certain that we will die,* and *it is uncertain when or how we will die.* The only surety we have, then, is this uncertainty about the hour of our death, which we seize on as the excuse to postpone facing death directly.

March

30

31

The Dalai Lama has said: 'There is no need for temples; no need for complicated philosophy. Our own brain, our own heart is our temple; my philosophy is kindness.'

April

1

2

3

April

4

5

6

While circumambulating the Great Stupa at
Bodh Gaya, the place where the Buddha
attained enlightenment, the Buddhist master
Atisha actually heard this statue of Tara
speaking. Her words inspired him to travel to
the island of Sumatra where he received the
complete teachings on compassion that were
no longer to be found in India.

April

7

8

9

10

11

If we look into our lives, we will see clearly how many unimportant tasks, so-called 'responsibilities' accumulate to fill them up. One master compares them to 'housekeeping in a dream.'

April

12

13

14

15

16

Tomorrow or the next life – which comes first, we never know.

April

17

18

19

20

21

I often compare the mind in meditation to a jar of muddy water: The more we leave the water without interfering or stirring it, the more the particles of dirt will sink to the bottom, letting the natural clarity of the water shine through.

April

22

23

24

25

26

So often we want happiness, but the very way we pursue it is so clumsy and unskillful that it brings only more sorrow. Usually we assume we must grasp in order to have something that will ensure our happiness.

April

27

28

29

April-May

30

1

'If we have lived before,' I'm often asked, 'why don't we remember it?' If we cannot remember what we were doing or thinking last Monday, how on earth do we imagine it would be easy, or normal, to remember what we were doing in a previous lifetime?

May

2

3

4

5

© Mark Tracy

The gentle compassionate gaze of the eyes of a
Buddha; from a statue at the temple of Dorjé
Gyaltsen, Boudanath, Nepal.

May

6

7

8

9

10

'Grief,' Rumi wrote, 'can be the garden of compassion. If you keep your heart open through everything, your pain can become your greatest ally in your life's search for love and wisdom.'

May

11

12

13

14

15

'When the all-pervading rays of the Buddha's compassion are focused through the magnifying glass of your faith and devotion, the flame of blessings blazes up in your being.'

DILGO KHYENTSE RINPOCHE

May

16

17

18

19

20

'It is our collective and individual responsibility
to protect and nurture the global family, to
support its weaker members, and to preserve and
tend to the environment in which we all live.'

THE DALAI LAMA

May

21

22

23

24

25

When someone is suffering and you find yourself at a loss to know how to help, put yourself unflinchingly in his or her place. Imagine as vividly as possible what *you* would be going through if you were suffering the same pain.

May

26

27

28

29

30

As Buddha said, 'What you are is what you have done, what you will be is what you do now.'

May-June

31

1

2

3

4

Jowo Shakyamuni, believed to have been made
during the lifetime of the Buddha, is the most
highly revered statue in Tibet. Beautifully
decorated with brocade and ornaments it is
installed as the central image in the Jokhang
temple, Lhasa. The temple remains the most
sacred place of pilgrimage in Tibet.

June

5

6

7

8

9

What is compassion? It is not simply a sense of sympathy or caring for the person suffering, not simply a warmth of heart toward the person before you, or a sharp clarity of recognition of their needs and pain, it is also a sustained and practical determination to do whatever is possible and necessary to help alleviate their suffering.

June

10

11

12

13

14

Looking into death needn't be frightening or morbid. Why not reflect on death when you are really inspired, relaxed and comfortable, lying in bed, or on holiday, or listening to music that particularly delights you?

June

15

16

17

18

19

It is important to reflect calmly, again and again, that *death is real and comes without warning*.

June

20

21

22

23

24

The turning point in any healing of alcoholics or drug addicts is when they admit their illness and ask for aid. In one way or another, we are all addicts of samsara; the moment when help can come for us is when we admit our addiction and simply ask.

June

25

26

27

28

29

Our task is to strike a balance, to find a middle way, to learn not to overstretch ourselves with extraneous activities and preoccupations, but to simplify our lives more and more. *The key to finding a happy balance in modern lives is simplicity.*

June-July

30

1

2

'Shelgrak Guru' is the renowned speaking
statue of Padmasambhava, the great tantric
master who established Buddhism in Tibet
during the 8th century. It now stands in the
Tramdruk Temple, Central Tibet.

July

3

4

5

6

7

The very nature of the mind is such that if you only leave it in its unaltered and natural state, it will find its true nature, which is bliss and clarity.

July

8

9

10

11

12

The realisation of impermanence is paradoxically the only thing we can hold onto, perhaps our only lasting possession. It is like the sky, or the earth. No matter how much everything around us may change or collapse, they endure.

July

13

14

15

16

17

'I am never far from those with faith, or even from those without it, though they do not see me. My children will always, always, be protected by my compassion.'

PADMASAMBHAVA

July

18

19

20

21

22

There is no substitute for regular practice, for only through real practice will we begin to taste unbrokenly the calm of our nature of mind and so be able to sustain the experience of it in our everyday lives.

July

23

24

25

26

27

Because the law of karma is inevitable and infallible, whenever we harm others, we are directly harming ourselves, and whenever we bring them happiness, we are bringing ourselves future happiness.

July

28

29

30

A mural from the White Monastery in Töling,
West Tibet, of Maha Prajnaparamita.
Prajnaparamita means 'Perfection of Wisdom ,'
a quality of the enlightened mind here
personified in the form of a female deity.

July-August

31

1

2

3

4

To calm your mind, go for a walk at dawn in the park, or watch the dew on a rose in a garden. Lie on the ground and gaze up into the sky, and let your mind expand into its spaciousness. Let the sky outside awake a sky inside your mind.

August

5

6

7

8

9

There would be no chance at all of getting to know death if it happened only once. But fortunately, life is nothing but a continuing dance of birth and death, a dance of change.

August

10

11

12

13

14

'If your mind is empty, it is always ready for anything; it is open to everything. In the beginner's mind there are many possibilities, in the expert's mind there are few.'

SUZUKI-ROSHI

August

15

16

17

18

19

Two people have been living in you all your life.
One is the ego, garrulous, demanding,
hysterical, calculating; the other is the hidden
spiritual being, whose still voice of wisdom you
have only rarely heard or attended to.

August

20

21

22

23

24

'He who binds to himself a Joy,
Does the winged life destroy;
He who kisses the Joy as it flies,
Lives in Eternity's sunrise.'

WILLIAM BLAKE

August

25

26

27

This beautifully ornamented seated figure of
Shakyamuni Buddha is situated in the
Gyantse Kumbum, Tibet. Shakyamuni is the
historical Buddha who attained enlightenment
at Bodh Gaya, India in 500 BC.

August

28

29

30

Aug-Sept

31

1

'If you want to know your past life, look into your present condition; if you want to know your future life, look at your present actions.'

PADMASAMBHAVA

September

2

3

4

5

6

Whatever you do, don't shut off your pain; accept your pain and remain vulnerable. However desperate you become, accept your pain as it is, because it is in fact trying to hand you a priceless gift: the chance of discovering, through spiritual practice, what lies behind sorrow.

September

7

8

9

10

11

All we need to do to receive direct help is to ask. Didn't Christ also say: 'Ask, and it shall be given you; seek and ye shall find; knock and it shall be opened unto you. Everyone that asketh receiveth; and he that seeketh findeth?' And yet asking is what we find hardest.

September

12

13

14

15

16

The absolute truth cannot be realised within the domain of the ordinary mind. And the path beyond the ordinary mind, all the great wisdom traditions have told us, is through the heart. This path of the heart is devotion.

September

17

18

19

20

21

Karma is not fatalistic or predetermined. Karma means *our* ability to create and to change. It is creative because we *can* determine how and why we act. We *can* change.

September

22

23

24

25

26

'Foolish selfish people are always thinking of themselves, and the result is negative. Wise selfish people think of others, help others as much as they can, and the result is that they too receive benefit.'

THE DALAI LAMA

September

27

28

29

Sept-Oct

30

1

Don't you notice that there are particular moments when you are naturally inspired to introspection? Work with them gently, for *these are the moments when you can go through a powerful experience, and your whole worldview can change quickly.*

October

2

3

4

A detail of the hands of Maitreya Buddha, the
future Buddha, from a statue in the Maitreya
chapel in the Jokhang temple, Lhasa. His
hands are held to his heart in a gesture
of teaching called 'Turning the Wheel
of the Dharma.'

October

5

6

7

8

9

When you meditate, there should be no effort to control, and no attempt to be peaceful. Don't be overly solemn or feel that you are taking part in some special ritual; let go even of the idea that you are meditating. Let your body remain as it is, and your breath as you find it.

October

10

11

12

13

14

My heartfelt advice to those in the depths of grief and despair after losing someone they dearly loved is to pray for help and strength and grace. Above all, look into your life to find ways of sharing your love more deeply with others now.

October

15

16

17

18

19

We all have the karma to meet one spiritual path or another, and I would encourage you, from the bottom of my heart, to follow with complete sincerity the path that inspires you most.

October

20

21

22

23

24

'So if we wish to die well, we must learn how to live well: Hoping for a peaceful death, we must cultivate peace in our mind, and in our way of life.'

THE DALAI LAMA

October

25

26

27

28

29

Imagine you are having difficulties with a loved one, such as your mother or father, husband or wife, lover or friend. Thinking of them as a real person, *exactly the same as you*, will open your heart to him or her and give you more insight into how to help.

Oct-Nov

30

31

1

2

This statue of Shakyamuni Buddha is located
in the main shrine room of the Mahabodhi
Stupa, directly to the east of the bodhi tree
under which Buddha manifested complete
enlightenment 2500 years ago.

November

3

4

5

6

7

Therefore, in meditation, you keep your eyes open, not closed. Instead of shutting out life, you remain open and at peace with everything. You leave all your senses – hearing, seeing, feeling – just open, naturally, as they are, without grasping after their perceptions.

November

8

9

10

11

12

13

November

14

15

16

17

18

Don't be in too much of a hurry to solve all your doubts and problems; as the masters say, 'Make haste slowly.' I always tell my students not to have unreasonable expectations, because it takes time for spiritual growth.

November

19

20

21

22

23

To work with changes now, in life: that is the real way to prepare for death. Life may be full of pain, suffering and difficulty, but all of these are opportunities handed to us to help us move toward an emotional acceptance of death.

November

24

25

26

27

28

What really matters is not just the practice of sitting but far more the state of mind you find yourself in after meditation. It is this calm and centred state of mind you should prolong through everything you do.

Nov-Dec

29

30

1

This statue of Avalokiteshvara is located in
the Drepung Monastery in Central Tibet.
Avalokiteshvara is the Bodhisattva of
Compassion, the enlightened being who takes
special care of Tibet and is so close to the
heart of the Tibetan people.

December

2

3

4

5

6

My master Dilgo Khyentse Rinpoche said: 'The more and more you listen, the more and more you hear; the more and more you hear, the deeper and deeper your understanding becomes.'

December

7

8

9

10

11

To train in compassion is to know that all beings are the same and suffer in similar ways, to honour all those who suffer, and to know that you are neither separate from nor superior to anyone.

December

12

13

14

15

16

The spiritual journey is one of continuous learning and purification. When you know this, you become humble. There is a famous Tibetan saying: 'Do not mistake understanding for realisation, and do not mistake realisation for liberation.'

December

17

18

19

20

21

22

December

23

24

25

26

27

There is a famous Zen saying, 'When I eat, I eat; when I sleep, I sleep.' To eat when you eat and sleep when you sleep means to be completely present in all your actions, with none of the distractions of ego to stop you being there. This is integration.

December

28

29

30

31